D1604901

Real Life Stories

NATIVE-AMERICAN LIFE

Jill Foran

— Weigl Publishers Inc. —

About *Native-American Life*

This book is based on the real life accounts of the people who settled the American West. History is brought to life through quotes from personal journals, letters to family back home, and historical records of those who traveled West to build a better life.

Published by Weigl Publishers Inc.
123 South Broad Street, Box 227
Mankato, MN 56002
USA

Web site: www.weigl.com

Library of Congress Cataloging-in-Publication Data

Foran, Jill.
  Native-American life / by Jill Foran.
      p. cm. -- (Real life stories series)
Includes index.
Summary: Briefly explores the history and culture of Native Americans, including first-hand accounts about family life, ceremonies, crafts, and hunting.
  ISBN 1-59036-080-X (lib. bdg. : alk. paper)
  1. Indians of North America--History--Juvenile literature. 2. Indians of North America--Social life and customs--Juvenile literature. [1. Indians of North America--History. 2. Indians of North America--Social life and customs.] I. Title. II. Series.
  E77.4 .F66 2003
  973.04'97--dc21

                                   2002012725

Printed in the United States of America
1 2 3 4 5 6 7 8 9 0   06 05 04 03 02

Photograph Credits

Cover: CORBIS/MAGMA; **Atwater Kent Museum:** page 1; **Corel Corporation:** page 5; **Denver Public Library Western History Department:** page 16 (X-33189); **Glenbow Archives:** pages 12/13 (NA-1481-257), 14 (NA-1811-18); **Minnesota State Historical Society:** pages 3 (E98R10), 10 (E98/R10), 22 (E97.1/R215); **Nativestock.com:** page 4; **photos courtesy National Archives of Canada:** pages 6 (C403), 21 (C41663); **State Historical Society of Wisconsin:** page 18 (Whi (X3) 47169); **Utah State Historical Society:** page 8 (#14497).

Project Coordinator Michael Lowry	**Copy Editor** Frances Purslow	**Layout** Terry Paulhus
Substantive Editor Christa Bedry	**Design** Virginia Boulay & Bryan Pezzi	**Photo Research** Dylan Kirk & Daorcey Le Bray

Contents

Love of the Land

Native Americans lived in North America long before the Europeans arrived. Native Americans belonged to many different **nations**. The nations developed over thousands of years. They had many **traditions**. All of the nations had one thing in common. They shared a great respect for nature. Native Americans lived in harmony with the land.

Native Americans in the Northeast lived in homes called wigwams. Wigwams were dome-shaped homes that were covered with tree bark or woven mats.

Real Life Stories

*"We have lived upon this land from days beyond history's records, far past any living memory, deep into the time of **legend**. The story of my people and the story of this place are one single story. We are always joined together."*

A Pueblo Elder

Different Ways of Life

Native Americans from different regions had different life styles. Some Native Americans were farmers. They lived in one place. They grew corn and other crops. Some Native Americans were hunters. They followed **prey**, such as buffalo and deer. Hunters believed that all life was holy. They believed that animals should only be killed when the need was great. Every part of an animal's body was used after it was killed.

Native Americans hunted and traveled on foot before they had horses. The Europeans brought the first horses to North America.

Real Life Stories

"When I was about 8 or 10 years old, I began to follow the chase … out on the prairies … wandered herds of deer, antelope, elk, and buffalo, to be [killed] when we needed them. Usually we hunted buffalo on horseback, killing them with arrows and spears. Their skins were used to make tepees and bedding; their flesh, to eat."

Geronimo

Role Playing

Family was very important to Native Americans. Grandparents, parents, and children all shared a close bond. Each family member played a certain role. Men were hunters and warriors. Women built and looked after the homes. Women also grew crops and gathered food. Children were given chores. They played games when their work was done. The children often acted out the roles of adults in these games.

Native-American women were responsible for raising the children.

Real Life Stories

"I tried to be like my mother ... I carried my doll on my back just as mothers carry their babies ... I had a little tepee that I pitched whenever my aunt pitched hers. It was made exactly like my aunt's, had the same number of poles, only of course my tepee was very small ... Once, several of us girls made ourselves a play village with our tiny tepees. Of course our children were dolls, and our horses dogs, and yet we managed to make our village look very real."

Pretty Shield

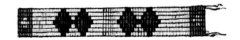

Arts and Crafts

Arts and crafts were an important part of Native-American life. Native-American artwork honored their **culture**. Native-American artists in the south painted **pictographs**. These paintings showed humans, animals, or special events. Artists from other areas made carvings out of wood, bone, and stone. Native-American groups from the Great Plains made clothes out of buffalo skins. They decorated their clothes with beads and porcupine quills.

Native Americans in the Northeast made baskets out of tree bark, grass, or corn stalks. What items could you make out of tree bark?

Real Life Stories

"In the old days they used to decorate their clothing and fancy articles with colored porcupine quills. Quillwork was a special craft and a woman had to be **initiated** *by an older lady before she could begin … the Blackfoot quillworker is supposed to follow a number of rules. For instance, it is said that quillworkers go blind if they ever throw a porcupine quill into a fire, or if they do quillwork at night."*

Ruth Little Bear

A Traditional Tepee

The types of homes built by the Native Americans varied from region to region. Some farming nations lived in houses made of wood and brush. Other nations lived in earth lodges. Earth lodges were made out of **sod**. Great Plains nations usually lived in tepees. Tepees were cone-shaped tents. They were roomy, **portable**, and easy to set up.

The tepee cover was made of buffalo skins. The skins were tied over a frame of wooden poles.

Family members, clothes, tools, weapons, and food could fit inside a tepee.

Wooden pegs attached the tepee cover to the ground.

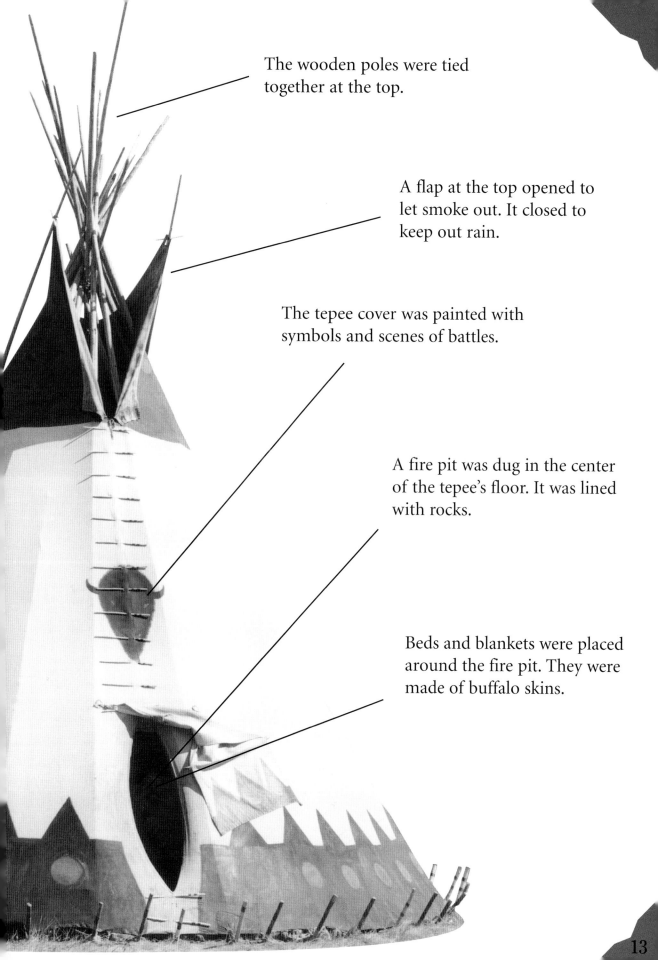

The wooden poles were tied together at the top.

A flap at the top opened to let smoke out. It closed to keep out rain.

The tepee cover was painted with symbols and scenes of battles.

A fire pit was dug in the center of the tepee's floor. It was lined with rocks.

Beds and blankets were placed around the fire pit. They were made of buffalo skins.

Storytelling

Many Native-American nations did not have a written language. They passed information from parents to children through storytelling. Storytellers told the history of a nation. Storytellers also taught the traditions and laws of their nations. This is how their traditions were kept alive. Native Americans remembered their past through stories.

Native Americans often used musical instruments, such as drums, to help tell stories.

Real Life Stories

"As we ate our evening meal around the fire, an older man recited the stories of our people. Sometimes my father recited these stories, or sometimes one of his warriors did; sometimes a visitor was given the honor. We heard these stories until we memorized them. The [storyteller] never [changed] one word … each account was … handed down word-for-word as it happened. Occasionally some child went to sleep during the recital, but I did not."

Asa Daklugie

Important Events

Native Americans held many gatherings each year. Each nation had its own ceremonies. Ceremonies are events that mark special occasions. Some ceremonies were held to heal the sick. Other ceremonies marked important stages of life. Ceremonies were performed to make sure hunting trips were successful. Many Native Americans also held ceremonies to give thanks for successful crops.

Ceremonies were an important part of Native-American life. What events do you celebrate in your life?

Real Life Stories

"Our people believed that before they planted a crop or started the important work of the new year they should hold a Bread Dance when the Great Spirit would be [asked] to bless the people and give them a [good] crop and a [successful], peaceful year … we looked forward to the spring Bread Dance, as to our most festive occasions. The Bread Dance really opened the festivities of spring and summer, when all nature seemed to be rejoicing and happy. Not until after this important ceremony would anyone venture to plant a crop of corn or [begin] any important work."

Thomas Wildcat Alford

Across North America

Many Native-American nations were living across North America when Christopher Columbus discovered the Americas in 1492. These nations lived in many different regions. For example, the Sioux lived on the Great Plains, and the Pueblo lived in the dry Southwest. The Chippewa lived in the Northeast.

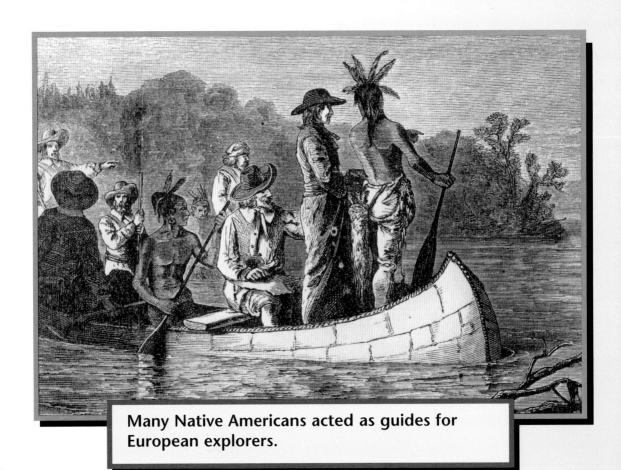

Many Native Americans acted as guides for European explorers.

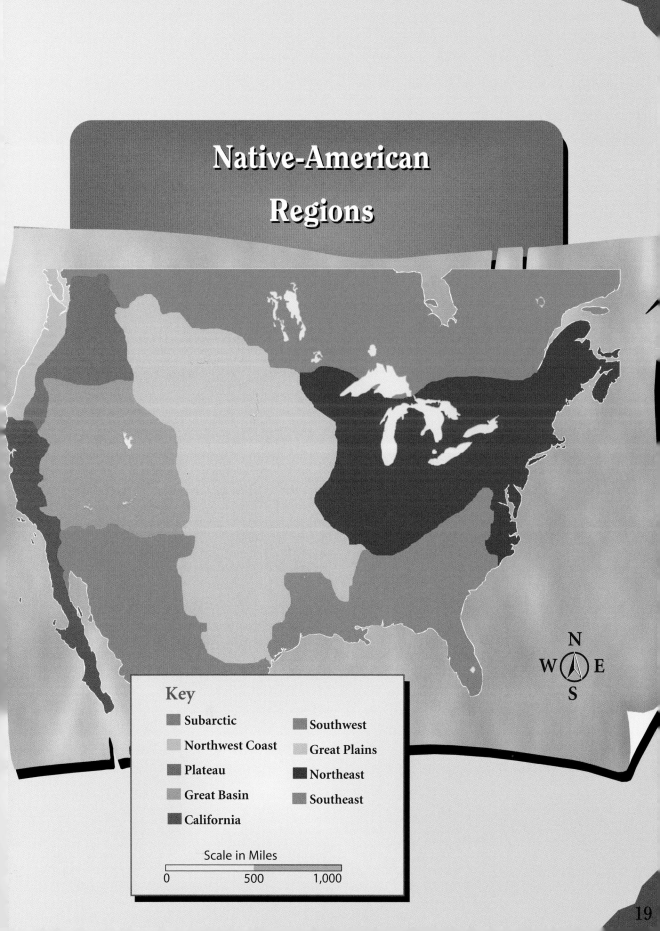

Native-American Regions

Key

- Subarctic
- Northwest Coast
- Plateau
- Great Basin
- California
- Southwest
- Great Plains
- Northeast
- Southeast

N
W E
S

Scale in Miles

0   500   1,000

Learning More about Native-American Life

To learn more about homesteading, you can borrow books from the library or surf the Internet.

Books

Ansary, Mir Tamim. *Plains Indians: Native Americans*. Chicago: Heinemann Library, 2001.

Green, Jen, *et al* (Ed). *The Encyclopedia of Ancient Americans: Explore the Wonders of the Aztec, Maya, Inca, North American & Arctic Peoples*. London: Southwater Publishing, 2001.

Web Sites

The First Americans
www.germantown.k12.il.us/html/intro.html
This Web site explores the many different Native-American cultures in North America.

Encarta
www.encarta.com
Enter the search words "Native American" into an online encyclopedia, such as Encarta.

Compare and Contrast

Life changed for the Native Americans when the Europeans arrived in North America. European explorers brought many goods with them. Native-American nations began to trade with the Europeans. They gave the Europeans food, furs, and traditional clothing. The Native Americans received guns, tools, and blankets in exchange. Below are pictures of tools and other items used by Native Americans. Use the Internet to research which items were used before the Europeans arrived. Then, find the items that were used after Europeans arrived.

What Have You Learned?

Based on what you have read, try to answer the following questions.

1 True or False? Many Native-American nations passed their traditions through storytelling.

2 From what type of animal skin was a tepee usually made?

a) horse
b) cow
c) buffalo
d) wolf

3

True or false?
A Bread Dance
honors the people
who make bread.

4

How were porcupine quills
used on the Great Plains?

a) to decorate clothing
b) to make weapons
c) to cook food
d) to build wigwams

5

What did Native
Americans use to help
tell stories?

a) books
b) sign language
c) writing
d) drums

6

True or false?
Native Americans
only used the skin
of the buffalo.

Answers

1. True
2. c
3. False. A Bread Dance was used to ask the Great Spirit for a successful crop and a peaceful year.
4. a
5. d
6. False. Native Americans used every part of an animal that was killed.

Words to Know

culture: behaviors and beliefs of a group of people

initiated: introduced to a new skill

legend: a popular story that cannot be proven to be true

nations: Native-American groups

pictographs: paintings or drawings on rock walls

portable: easily carried or moved

prey: animals that are hunted and killed for food

sod: piece of grassy ground

traditions: the beliefs and behaviors that are passed down from parents to children

Index